YOU CAN TEACH YOURSELF®
GOSPEL PIANO

By Gail Smith

W9-CPJ-648

CD CONTENTS*

1 Introduction (1:47)
2 Chapter 1 (1:45)
3 Quiz & Time Signatures (:45)
4 Middle C (:46)
5 D Song & E Song (:24)
6 F Song & G Song (:18)
7 A Song & B Song (:27)
8 Introducing Rests (:38)
9 Introducing Musical Terms (:12)
10 Chapter 2 (1:10)
11 Alleluia, Sing to Jesus (:43)
12 When I Survey the Wondrous Cross (:36)
13 Come, Thou Almighty King (:29)
14 Chapter 3 (:44)
15 Train Up a Child & Alleluia (:35)
16 The Trinity (:29)
17 God Is So Good (:41)
18 Inversions & Trust (:40)
19 C Chord Inversions (1:02)
20 Halleluia (:37)
21 When the Saints Go Marching In (:22)
22 When the... Transposed to G (:37)
23 When I Survey the Wondrous Cross (1:34)
24 Joyful, Joyful We Adore Thee (:24)
25 Artillary Song (Sharps, Flats, & Naturals) (1:58)
26 Stages of Development:
   Savior, Like a Shepherd Lead Us (1:05)
27 Do Lord (Four Gospel Styles) (:57)
28 Chapter 4 (:38)
29 Amazing Grace & The First Noel (1:01)
30 Tallis's Canon (Round Styles & Examples) (1:16)
31 Chapter 5 (2:27)
32 Halleluia (:40)

33 Stand Up, Stand Up for Jesus (:52)
34 My Jesus, I Love Thee (:41)
35 Come, Thou Almighty King (:33)
36 Chapter 6 (1:26)
37 O the Deep, Deep Love of Jesus (:38)
38 Love Lifted Me (:35)
39 Rock of Ages (:32)
40 For the Beauty of the Earth (:39)
41 Jesus, Lover of My Soul (:50)
42 Come, Thou Fount of Every Blessing (:41)
43 Chapter 7 (:24)
44 88 Left-Hand Patterns: 1-5 (:21)
45 88 Left-Hand Patterns: 6-10 (:19)
46 88 Left-Hand Patterns: 11-15 (:22)
47 88 Left-Hand Patterns: 16-20 (:19)
48 88 Left-Hand Patterns: 21-25 (:20)
49 88 Left-Hand Patterns: 26-30 (:22)
50 88 Left-Hand Patterns: 31-35 (:18)
51 88 Left-Hand Patterns: 36-40 (:19)
52 88 Left-Hand Patterns: 41-45 (:22)
53 88 Left-Hand Patterns: 46-50 (:27)
54 88 Left-Hand Patterns: 51-55 (:22)
55 88 Left-Hand Patterns: 56-60 (:21)
56 88 Left-Hand Patterns: 61-65 (:23)
57 88 Left-Hand Patterns: 66-70 (:21)
58 88 Left-Hand Patterns: 71-75 (:21)
59 88 Left-Hand Patterns: 76-80 (:19)
60 88 Left-Hand Patterns: 81-88 (:38)
61 The Battle Hymn of the Republic (:20)
62 He's Got the Whole World in His Hands (:18)
63 He Is Lord (:23)
64 Jesus Loves Me (:42)
65 Just as I Am (:40)

66 When the Roll Is Called (:44)
67 Nothing But the Blood (:39)
68 Standing on the Promises (:40)
69 Glory to His Name (:35)
70 My Country, 'Tis of Thee (:40)
71 America the Beautiful (:42)
72 Pass Me Not, O Gentle Savior (:45)
73 Softly and Tenderly (:57)
74 Morning Song (:34)
75 Amazing Grace (:33)
76 At Calvary (:48)
77 Silent Night (:49)
78 Away in a Manger (:35)
79 The First Noel (:44)
80 What Child Is This (:26)
81 Trust and Obey (:41)
82 Holy, Holy, Holy (:46)
83 Chapter 8 (1:13)
84 Blest Be the Tie That Binds (Short Meter) (:35)
85 The Doxology (Long Meter) (:45)
86 Chapter 9 (:33)
87 The Lord's My Shepherd, I'll Not Want (:25)
88 Oh, How I Love Jesus (:28)
89 Jesus Never Fails (:27)
90 Only Trust Him (:52)
91 Day by Day Medley (1:02)
92 Like a River Glorious (2:28)
93 My Jesus I Love Thee (:45)
94 What a Friend (:46)
95 Angels We Have Heard on High (:55)
96 Jesus, What a Friend of Sinners (1:34)
97 Abide with Me (1:12)
98 Four-Beat Fills & Onward Christian Soldiers (1:01)
99 Chapter 10: Special Effects & Conclusion (2:05)

*This book is available as a book only or as a book/compact disc configuration.

CHECK OUT CREATIVE KEYBOARD'S _FREE WEBZINE_ @ www.creativekeyboard.com

If you have purchased the book only, a recording (97099CD) of the music in this book is now available. The publisher strongly recommends the use of this resource along with the text to insure accuracy of interpretation and ease in learning.

Visit us on the Web at www.melbay.com — E-mail us at email@melbay.com

1 2 3 4 5 6 7 8 9 0

SONG TITLES

WARNING: MUSICAL DANGER IF YOU DON'T READ THIS

Pretending that the person using this book has no previous musical knowledge absolutely scares me! I wish I could personally teach everyone to play Gospel Piano step by step, but since that is not humanly possible, I'm hoping that you will be able to learn to play by going through each page of this book very carefully, all by yourself.

Here are some important things to keep in mind:

The way to begin a musical education is to listen to music around you. Robert Schumann begins his list of 64 rules for young musicians by saying, "The cultivation of the ear is of the greatest importance.

Music employs certain symbols, such as lines, spaces, time signatures, key signatures, clefs, notes, rests, bars, accent marks and tempo markings. There is a whole musical vocabulary out there for you to learn, but just think, It is the Universal language.

The foundation to all skills is developing correct habits. There is no such thing as practice making perfect unless we practice playing perfect. Habit is a powerful force; each time we repeat a note correctly it will become a chain of correct notes. Avoid mistakes by going slowly the first time. The first time largely determines all subsequent times. As a sheet of paper will bend a second and a third time where it was first creased, so try to play the correct note with the correct finger from the beginning. Make it a habit to play slow and play right. Success is assured if you concentrate, practice and have the desire to learn.

Devote a little time every day to practicing the piano. Your fingers will need to adjust to exercise. As your finger muscles get stronger you will be able to play the piano longer. Success comes with time and labor. If you go on patiently, each day you will see progress. "Great men take short steps carefully, no matter how rapidly they are to go," wrote Robert Schumann.

Your desire to play the piano will transform that possibility into reality! Yes, where there's a will there's a way.

GAIL SMITH

Chapter 1
Getting Started

There are seven days in a week. There are seven musical notes. Here they are:

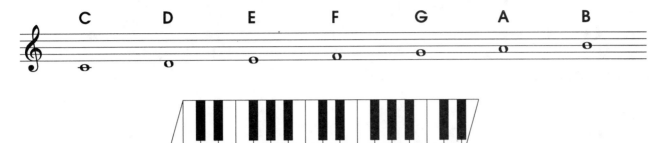

The musical letters repeat over and over as you go up the keyboard. We will learn them one at a time.

Introducing the Twelve Half-Steps

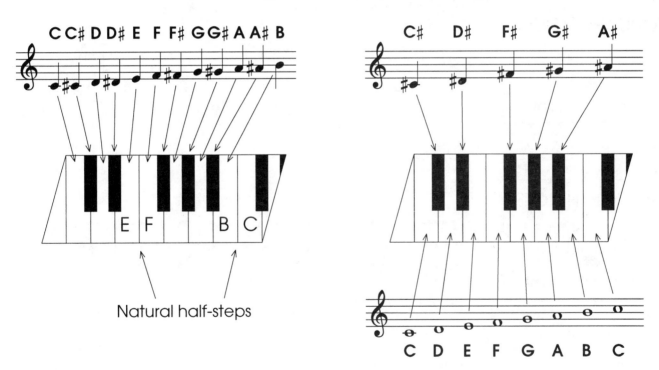

Natural half-steps

Just as there are twelve months in each year, there are twelve half-steps on the piano in one octave. They repeat over and over again.

Find the groups of two black keys. Next play the groups of three black keys. Then go from the lowest note on your piano and play each key, white and black, till you reach the top. How many keys were there?

Introducing Note I.D.'s

Credit Card

A WHOLE NOTE
𝅝
Value: 4 counts

A HALF NOTE
Value: 2 counts

A QUARTER NOTE
Value: 1 count

AN EIGHTH NOTE
♪
Value: 1/2 count

Time Line

𝅝 | 𝅝 | 𝅝 | 𝅝 |
1 2 3 4 1 2 3 4 1 2 3 4 1 2 3 4

𝅗𝅥 𝅗𝅥 | 𝅗𝅥 𝅗𝅥 | 𝅗𝅥 𝅗𝅥 | 𝅗𝅥 𝅗𝅥 |
1 2 3 4 1 2 3 4 1 2 3 4 1 2 3 4

♩ ♩ ♩ ♩ | ♩ ♩ ♩ ♩ | ♩ ♩ ♩ ♩ | ♩ ♩ ♩ ♩ |
1 2 3 4 1 2 3 4 1 2 3 4 1 2 3 4

♫♫♫♫ | ♫♫♪♪♪ | ♫♫♫♫ | ♪♪♪♫♪♪ |
1+2+3+4+ 1+2+3 + 4 + 1+2+3+4+ 1+2 + 3+4 +

Introducing the Lines and Spaces

Notes may be placed on lines, like these:

Notes may be placed on spaces, like these:

The Treble Clef
Right Hand
Higher Notes

The Bass Clef
Left Hand
Lower Notes

See the difference?

Here's a little quiz. Look at each note and tell if it is on a space or on a line. Write "S" for Space or "L" for Line in the box under the note.

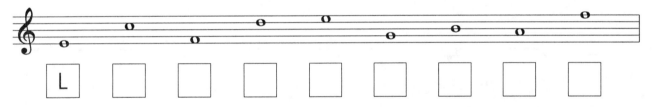

| L | | | | | | | | |

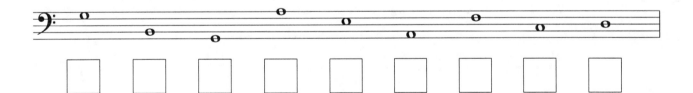

| | | | | | | | | |

The Gospel In a Noteshell

Fill in the missing letters by naming the notes. Identify the line or space. Look at the chart on the bottom of the page for help.

John 3:16

For _ o _ so lov _ _ th _ worl_

th_t H_ _ _v_ his only _ _ _ott_n

son th_t whoso_v_r _ _li_v_th

in Him shoul_ not p_rish

_ut h_v_ _v_rl_stin_ li_ _

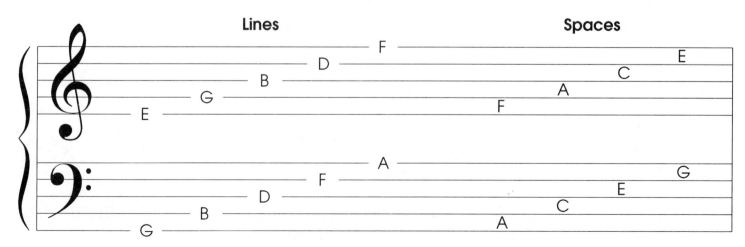

Lines

F
D
B
G
E

Spaces

E
C
A
F

A
F
D
B
G

G
E
C
A

8

Introducing Time Signatures

Each measure of music has a specified number of **beats** or **counts**. The numbers at the beginning of a piece of study will indicate **how many beats** in a measure, and **what kind of a note** gets a beat.

  $\begin{matrix} 2 \\ 4 \end{matrix}$ Top number = 2 beats in each measure.
Bottom number = A quarter note (♩) gets one beat.

  $\begin{matrix} 3 \\ 4 \end{matrix}$ Top number = 3 beats in each measure.
Bottom number = A quarter note (♩) gets one beat.

  $\begin{matrix} 4 \\ 4 \end{matrix}$ Top number = 4 beats in each measure.
Bottom number = A quarter note (♩) gets one beat.

  $\begin{matrix} 6 \\ 8 \end{matrix}$ Top number = 6 beats in each measure.
Bottom number = An eighth note (♪) gets one beat.

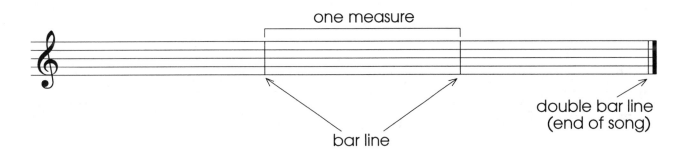

From one bar line to another is a full measure. At the beginning of each song, the Time Signature will appear. Watch for it!

Introducing the Note C

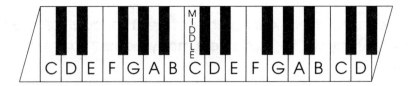

The note at the very top of the piano with 88 keys is a C. Middle C is the fourth C going up from the left side of the piano.

Find and play all the C's.

This is Middle C as a whole note:

This is Middle C as a dotted half note:

This is Middle C as a half note:

This is Middle C as a quarter note:

This is Middle C as a running eighth note:

C Song

Matthew 11:28   Gail Smith

Come un - to me all ye that la - bour and

are hea - vy la - den, and I will give you rest.

Introducing the Note D

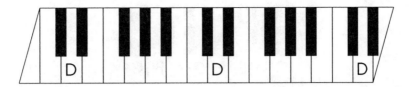

Between the two black keys on the piano you'll find the note D.

Find and play all seven D's on the piano.

D is about to drop off the staff.

D Song

Gail Smith

Do un - to oth - ers as

you would have them do to you.

Introducing the Note E

The note on the first line in the treble clef is E.

1   2   3   4   5   6   7   8   9   10

Play all ten E's

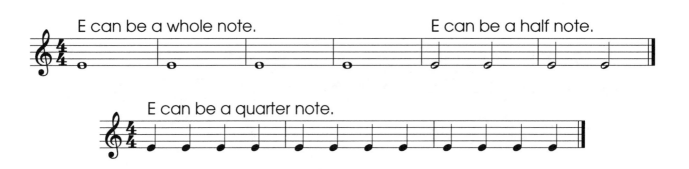

E can be a whole note.   E can be a half note.

E can be a quarter note.

E Song

James 1:19b   Gail Smith

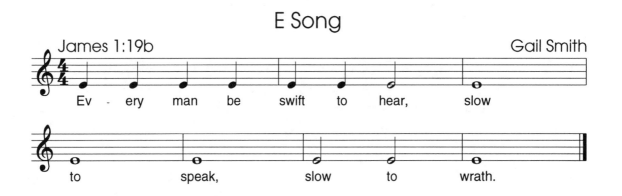

Ev - ery man be swift to hear, slow

to speak, slow to wrath.

Introducing the Note F

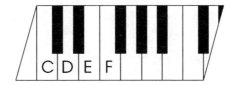

F is the first note in a space.

Count and play:

1 2 3 4

1 2 3 4

1 2 3 4

F Song

Matthew 4:19   Gail Smith

Fol - low me,   and   I   will   make   you   fish - ers   of   men.

Introducing the Note G

The note on the second line in the treble clef is G.

Play these ten notes.

whole note   half notes   quarter notes

Let's review the five white-key notes that we've learned so far.

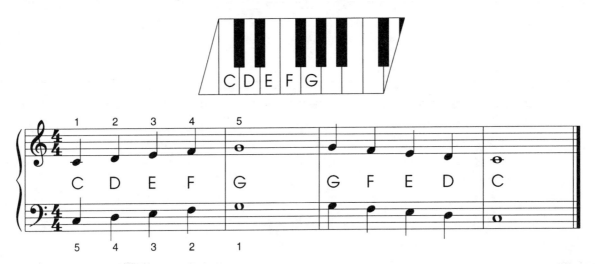

G Song

Psalm 96:8

Gail Smith

Give un - to the Lord _____ the glo - ry due his name.

Introducing the Note A

The note on the second space in the treble clef is A.

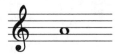

In the bass clef, the note A is on the fifth line.

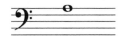

| 1 | 2 | 3 | 4 | 5 | 6 | 7 | 8 | 9 | 10 |

Play these ten A's.

The Left Hand Plays A

Gail Smith

A - men   A - men   A - men   A - men

Here is the left-hand A   The right-hand A

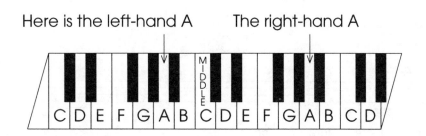

Introducing the Note B

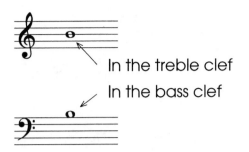

In the treble clef

In the bass clef

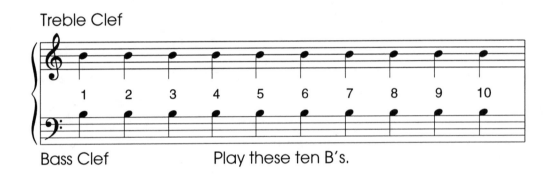

There are 8 B's on the piano. Find them.

Treble Clef

Bass Clef   Play these ten B's.

B Song

Matthew 5:48   Gail Smith

Be ye there - fore per - fect, ev - en as your

Fa - ther which is in hea - ven is per - fect.

16

Introducing Rests

Table of Rest Signs

| Whole Rest | ▬ | Quarter Rest | 𝄽 |
| Half Rest | ▬ | Eighth Rest | 𝄾 |

The Sabbath

Genesis 2:3

And God blessed the seventh day and made it
holy, because on it he rested from all the
work of creating that he had done

Gail Smith

pppp   *play super soft*

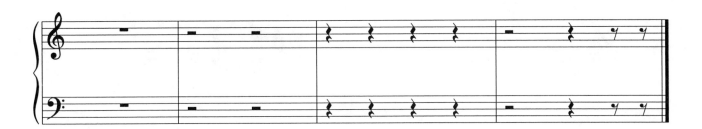

Introducing Dynamics

A Message In Song

The crescendo sign means to gradually play louder.

soft ＿＿＿＿＿ *loud*

John 3:30   Gail Smith

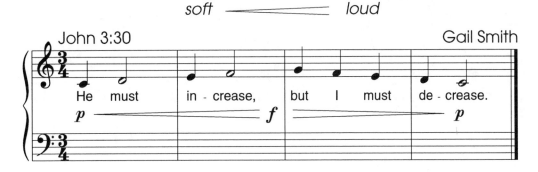

He must in - crease, but I must de - crease.

The decrescendo sign means to gradually play softer.

loud ＿＿＿＿＿ *soft*

Introducing Musical Terms

Accidentals

There are signs called accidentals which, when placed before a note, alter the pitch of the note.

♯	**Sharp**	Raises pitch a half-step
♭	**Flat**	Lowers pitch a half-step
𝄪	**Double-Sharp**	Raises pitch two half-steps, or one whole-step
♭♭	**Double-Flat**	Lowers pitch two half-steps, or one whole-step
♮	**Natural**	Cancels a sharp or a flat

Enharmonics

C sharp and D flat are enharmonics: they are the same note.

Both notes are located right here.

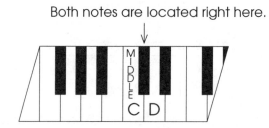

Other Terms

rit.	**Ritard**	Slow down
𝄐	**Fermata**	Hold on
sub.	**Subito**	Suddenly
◁═══	**Crescendo**	Gradually get louder
∧ or >	**Accent**	Play or sing stronger on that note
f or *ff*	**Forte**	Play or sing loud
p or *f*	**Piano**	Play or sing softly

For Your Information
Notes and Rests

Whole		Half		Quarter		Eighth		Sixteenth	
note	rest	note	rest	note	rest	note	rest	note	rest

Symbols

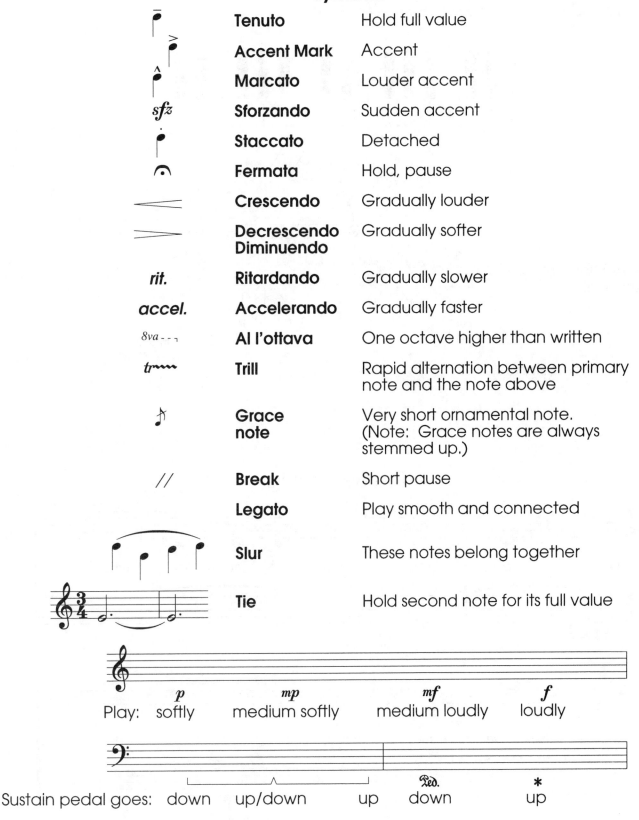

	Tenuto	Hold full value
	Accent Mark	Accent
	Marcato	Louder accent
sfz	**Sforzando**	Sudden accent
	Staccato	Detached
	Fermata	Hold, pause
	Crescendo	Gradually louder
	Decrescendo Diminuendo	Gradually softer
rit.	**Ritardando**	Gradually slower
accel.	**Accelerando**	Gradually faster
8va - - ¬	**Al l'ottava**	One octave higher than written
tr~~~	**Trill**	Rapid alternation between primary note and the note above
	Grace note	Very short ornamental note. (Note: Grace notes are always stemmed up.)
//	**Break**	Short pause
	Legato	Play smooth and connected
	Slur	These notes belong together
	Tie	Hold second note for its full value

Play: *p* softly   *mp* medium softly   *mf* medium loudly   *f* loudly

Sustain pedal goes: down   up/down   up   down   up

19

Chapter 2
Learning to Play Songs in the Five-Finger Position of the Key of C Major

The following songs are in the 5-finger position.

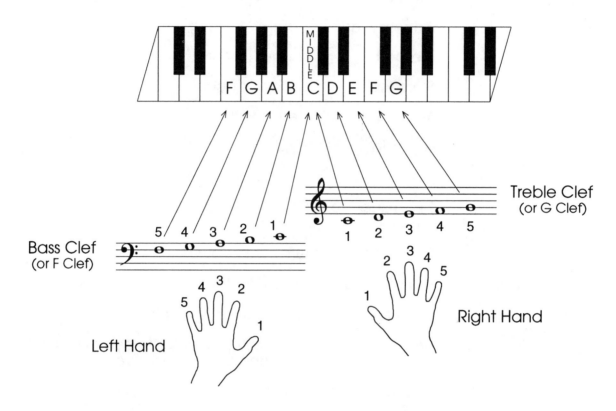

In The Beginning

Gail Smith

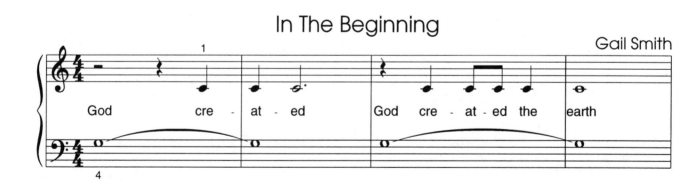

God   cre - at - ed   God   cre - at - ed the   earth

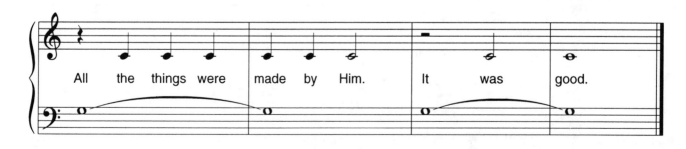

All   the   things   were   made   by   Him.   It   was   good.

He Cares

I Peter 5:7

Gail Smith

Cast - ing all your care u - pon Him, for he car - eth for you

The Just

Romans 1:17b

Gail Smith

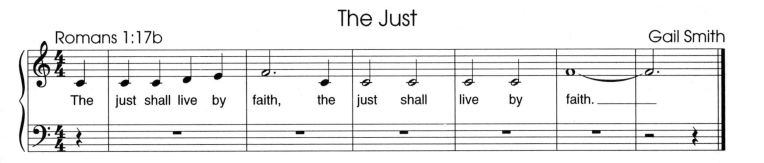

The just shall live by faith, the just shall live by faith.____

The Lord Is My Shepherd

Psalm 23:1,2

Gail Smith

The Lord is my Shep - herd I shall not

want. He mak - eth me to lie down in green

pas - tures: He lead - eth me be - side the still wa - ters.

Alleluia, Sing To Jesus

Arr. by Gail Smith

When I Survey The Wondrous Cross

arr. by Gail Smith

Come, Thou Almighty King

arr. by Gail Smith

Chapter 3
Learning to Play a Chord in the Left Hand

A **melody** is a succession of single tones.
A **chord** is a combination of tones sounded together.
A **triad** is a three-note chord.

In each of the following gospel songs you will play the melody and add one of these chords to the left hand.

Go back to this chart of chords to find the chord used in each song till you can play them without looking.

The dot shows the spot where the chord is on the piano.

Introducing Chords

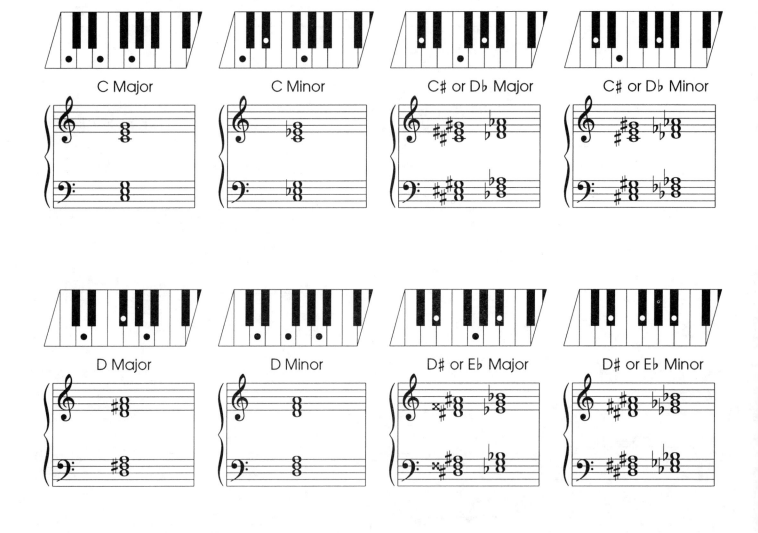

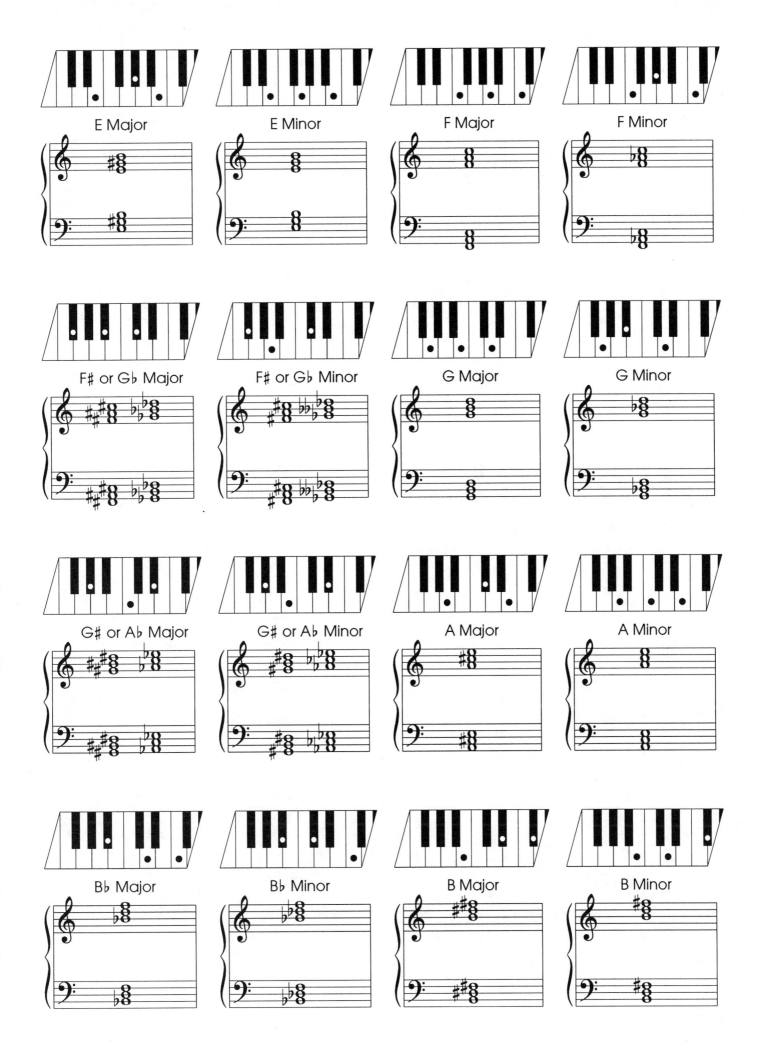

Train Up A Child

Proverbs 22:6

Gail Smith

Train up a child in the way he should go, and

when he is old he will not de - part from it.

Left-hand chord

Alleluia

Gail Smith

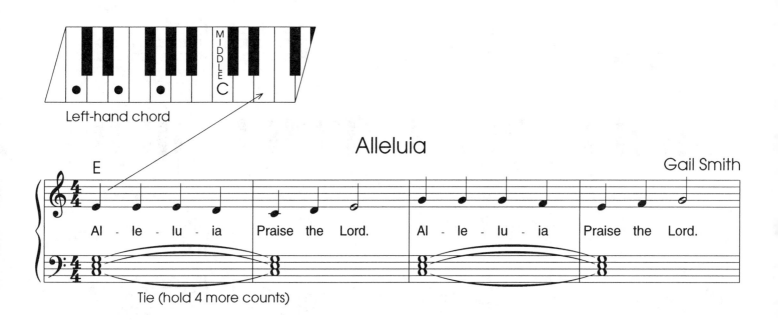

Al - le - lu - ia Praise the Lord. Al - le - lu - ia Praise the Lord.

Tie (hold 4 more counts)

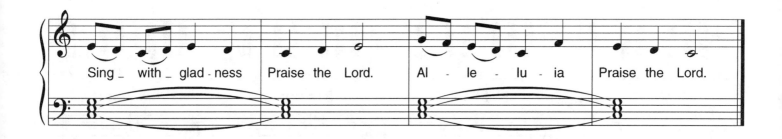

Sing _ with _ glad - ness Praise the Lord. Al - le - lu - ia Praise the Lord.

Introducing Triads

A triad has three notes.

F Chord

The Trinity

Gail Smith

Praise to the Fa - ther, Praise to the Son.

F chord

Praise the Ho - ly Spir - it Three in One.

Praise to the Fa - ther, Praise to the Son.

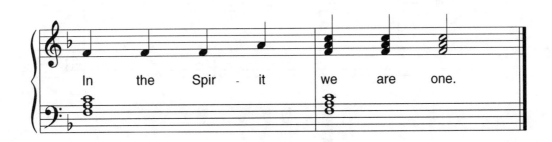

In the Spir - it we are one.

27

God Is So Good

This is the easiest Gospel song.

It is in the key of C. There are no sharps or flats in the key of C.

The melody in this song has only five notes:
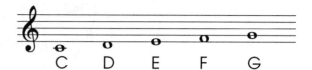
C   D   E   F   G

The 3 major chords in the key of C

First practice the C scale:

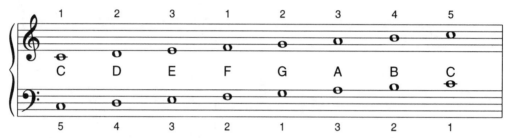

Now play and count the melody:

God Is So Good

F Chord (2nd Inversion)

Trust

Gail Smith

Trust in the Lord when you are stressed.

C chord   G chord

All will be well, you will be blessed.

Play the song again using the G chord inversion. It saves a big jump.

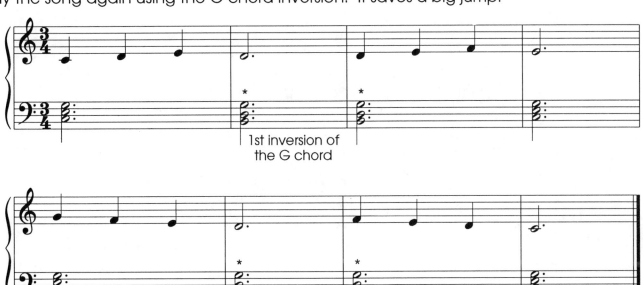

1st inversion of
the G chord

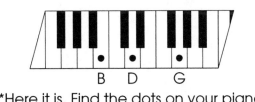

B   D   G

*Here it is. Find the dots on your piano

G Chord and Inversions

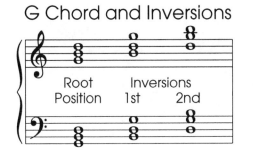

Root   Inversions
Position   1st   2nd

C Chord Inversions

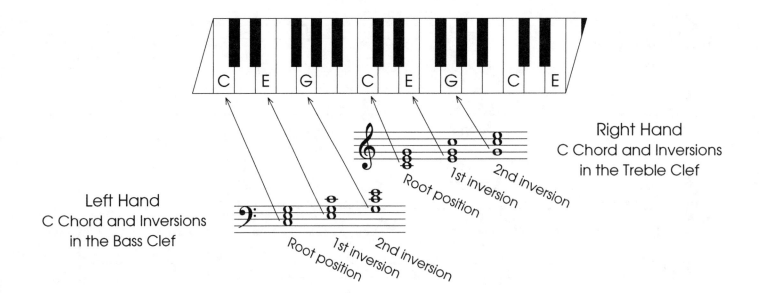

Left Hand
C Chord and Inversions
in the Bass Clef

Right Hand
C Chord and Inversions
in the Treble Clef

Example of a Triad and Inversions

G - 5	C - 1	E - 3
E - 3	G - 5	C - 1
C - 1	E - 3	G - 5
Root Position	First Inversion	Second Inversion

Chords in G

These are the chords in the key of G:

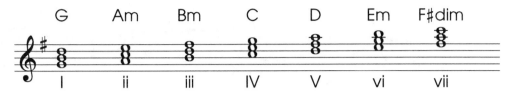

In chord names "m" means "minor" and "dim" means "diminished".

Halleluia

31

When The Saints Go Marching In
(with simple chords in the left hand)

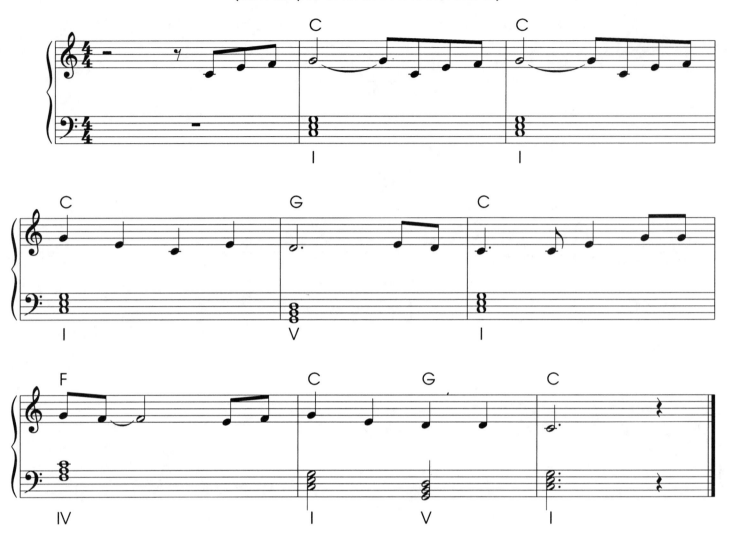

When The Saints Go Marching In

(transposed to the key of G)

arr. by Gail Smith

Intervals*:   2nd 3rd 4th 5th

* An **interval** is the distance between two notes. These are 4 examples:

** C chord in the 2nd **inversion**.

Here is the C chord with the inversions:

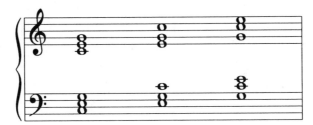

When I Survey The Wondrous Cross

Lowell Mason

A Tie

Hold this chord → → → → → → thru this measure.

Now here's the same song by Lowell Mason in the key of F. This means that every B note in the song is played a half-step lower, so you must use a black key on the piano.

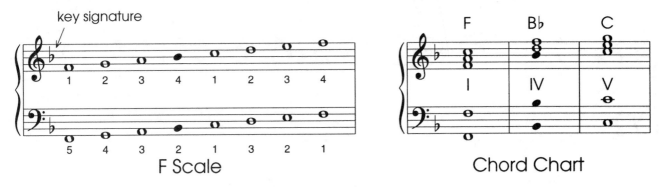

key signature

1 2 3 4 1 2 3 4

5 4 3 2 1 3 2 1

F Scale

F   Bb   C

I   IV   V

Chord Chart

1. Play the melody and count.
2. Play the scale.
3. Play the chords used in this song.

Note: With simple melodies the right hand can add an interval of a 6th below the melody as written. This melody has just four notes and uses a 5th tone only once. The left hand is playing a single octave note of the chord.

When I Survey The Wondrous Cross

Lowell Mason
arr. by Gail Smith

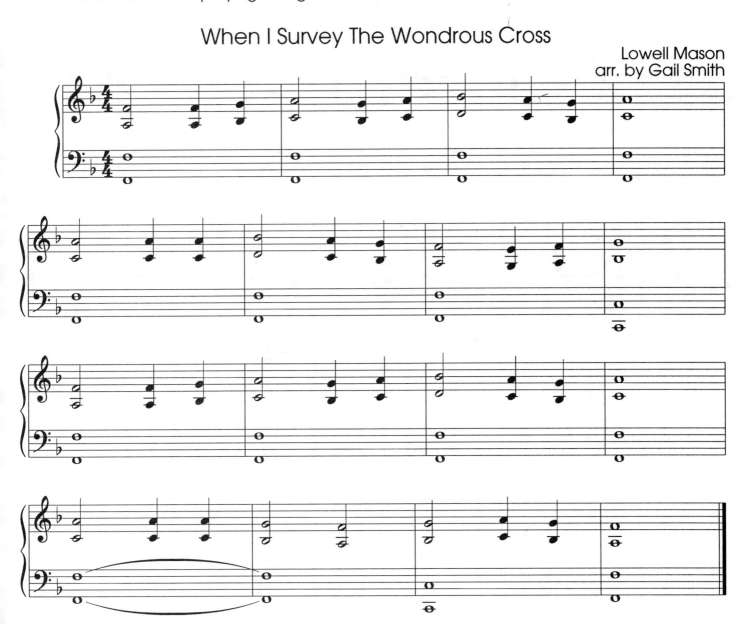

Joyful, Joyful We Adore Thee

Beethoven
arr. by Gail Smith

Artillary Song

This chorus is in the key of C. There are accidentals in this song. Accidentals are added flats (♭), sharps (♯), and natural marks (♮) that are not found in the key signature.

Review of Sharps, Flats, and Naturals

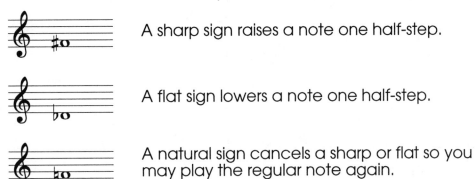

A sharp sign raises a note one half-step.

A flat sign lowers a note one half-step.

A natural sign cancels a sharp or flat so you may play the regular note again.

Watch for the accidentals in this song.

Artillary Song

37

In the following arrangement of the same song, the left-hand accompaniment uses this pattern of the chord note followed by a broken chord:

Artillary Song

Jesus Saves

Jesus Saves

39

Jesus Saves

Savior, Like A Shepherd Lead Us

Stages of Development

1. Learn melody.
2. Play melody with simple chords.
3. Add a third below the melody note to harmonize.
4. Use broken chord accompaniment in the left hand.

Savior, Like A Shepherd Lead Us

William Bradbury

This gospel song is in the key of C. In the next arrangement, the right hand is harmonized with an interval of a third below the melody note:

You may also try an octave with the third as shown:

The left hand plays broken chords using quarter-notes and half-notes:

Savior, Like A Shepherd Lead Us

William Bradbury
arr. by Gail Smith

Do Lord

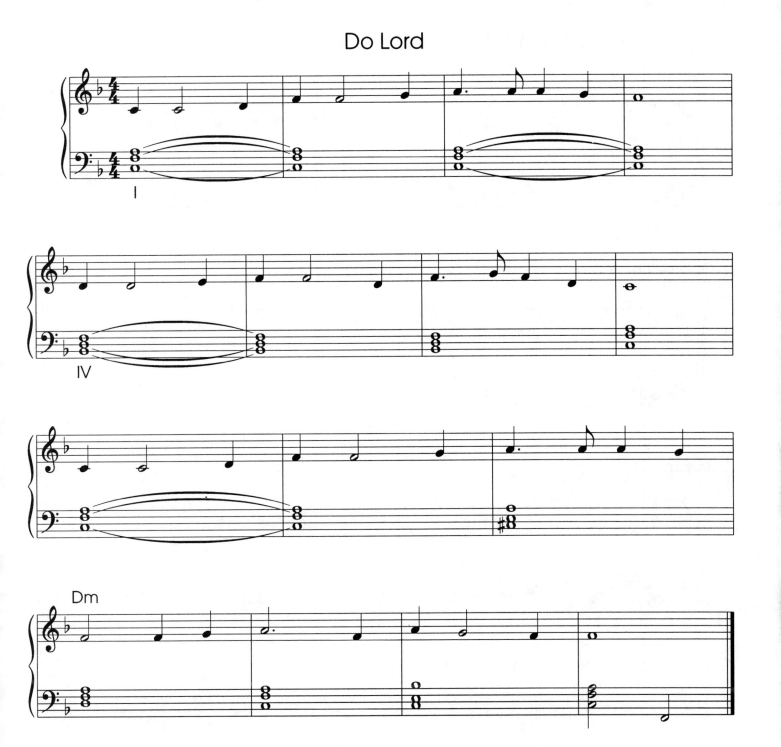

43

Following are four gospel styles to use with "Do Lord":

1. Broken chord:

2. Octave first, then chord:

3. Broken octave

4. Harmonic intervals of a 5th and a 6th:

44

Chapter 4
Playing Rounds

You may play the same melody in both hands. Start the melody over, coming in the next measure.

Play each hand separately first.

When *8va* appears, you play those notes an octave higher than written.

Sing A New Song
Isaiah 55:9
For as the heavens are higher than the earth,
so are my ways higher than your ways,
and my thoughts than your thoughts.

Gail Smith

Amazing Grace

As a Round

John Newton

The First Noel

English Carol

Tallis's Canon

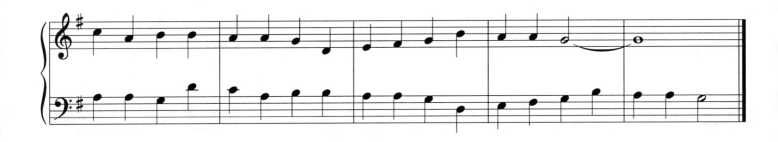

There are two ways to play a round. One way is to the have the melody in the treble start first. The other is to have the bass start as Leader. Here are both ways:

My Shepherd Will Supply My Need

American Melody
arr. by Gail Smith

My Shepherd Will Supply My Need

Chapter 5
Left-Hand Fill for Chord Progressions

It is very important to understand that every key has seven chords that belong to it.

These are the seven chords in the key of C:

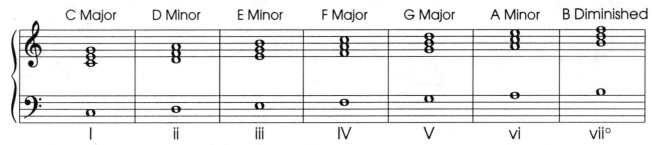

In playing gospel songs, we often use only the I, IV, and V chords. These three chords are the major chords in every major key. The three minor chords are ii, iii, and vi.

Play all these chords and listen to each different sound.

In the key of C, the major chords are C, F, and G. The minor chords are Dm, Em, and Am.

In "Left-Hand Fills for Basic Chord Progressions", only the Roman numerals are given. So, start thinking in those terms as well as remembering that a V chord is G in the key of C.

Here is a chart with the names and numbers of every major key. Each key has seven chords.

key	I	ii	iii	IV	V	vi	vii°
C	C	Dm	Em	F	G	Am	Bdim
G	G	Am	Bm	C	D	Em	F#dim
D	D	Em	F#m	G	A	Bm	C#dim
A	A	Bm	C#m	D	E	F#m	G#dim
E	E	F#m	G#m	A	B	C#m	D#dim
B	B	C#m	D#m	E	F#	G#m	A#dim
Gb	Gb	Abm	Bbm	Cb	Db	Ebm	Fdim
Db	Db	Ebm	Fm	Gb	Ab	Bbm	Cdim
Ab	Ab	Bbm	Cm	Db	Eb	Fm	Gdim
Eb	Eb	Fm	Gm	Ab	Bb	Cm	Ddim
Bb	Bb	Cm	Dm	Eb	F	Gm	Adim
F	F	Gm	Am	Bb	C	Dm	Edim

The Fill Chart on the next page helps you link all the chords in the left hand, giving you the "gospel sound."

Left-Hand Fills
for Basic Chord Progressions

Gail Smith

Using Left-Hand Fills for
Numbered Basic Chord Progressions

In the example below, "God Is So Good," the chords are:

C   G   G   C   C   F   G   C

Using the Fill Chart the left hand was filled in with the appropriate chord progression:

I   V   V   I   I   IV   V   I

God Is So Good

For help in modulating, you will find this book useful:

Halleluia

Perhaps you are wondering . . .

1. Question: Why are there only three beats at the end of this song?

   Answer: Beat 4 is at the beginning, and when there is a "pickup" beat at the beginning, you deduct the amount of that beat from the end.

2. Question: Why are there two lines at the end of the song?

   Answer: Each measure is separated from its neighbor by one line, but at the end there are two lines so you know it is the end.

3. Question: Why are there sharps at the beginning of the lines?

   Answer: This is the **key signature** and tells you that every F in the song will be sharped (raised a half step). The sharp must appear at the beginning of each line for the song to remain in the key of G.

53

Using the "Left-Hand Fills for Basic Chord Progressions" chart on pg. 51, write out the left hand for this hymn:

Stand Up, Stand Up For Jesus

George Webb

This is how it should look:

Stand Up, Stand Up For Jesus

George Webb

55

My Jesus, I Love Thee

A. J. Gordon
arr. by Gail Smith

Come, Thou Almighty King

arr. by Gail Smith

Chapter 6

In the following gospel songs, the phrases are marked A B etc. so that you may identify the repeated phrases. The songs are in the following form:

"Brethren, We Have Met To Worship"	A A B A
"O The Deep, Deep Love Of Jesus"	A A B A
"Love Lifted Me"	A B A B
"Rock Of Ages"	A A B
"For The Beauty Of The Earth"	A A B
"Jesus, Lover Of My Soul"	A A B A
"Come, Thou Fount Of Every Blessing"	A A B A

Here are some ideas for playing repeated phrases. A phrase may be repeated:
1. Identically
2. With embellishment
3. With a change of harmony
4. With a change of style of accompaniment
5. With a change of register
6. With a change of color

One of the basic ideas in musical form is that of symmetry or balance. As a rule, the initial phrase of a hymn is balanced by an answering phrase; the first is called the antecedent phrase, the second, the consequent phrase. The first phrase states a musical idea, and the second follows in consequence. These two related phrases are called a period. A double period consists of four phrases.

The following is an example of a double period (16 measures):

There is no strict rule as to phrase length: three-measure and five-measure phrases do occur in hymns. The following hymn phrases are examples of some irregular phrases:

2-measure phrase

3-measure phrase

4-measure phrase

5-measure phrase

Brethren, We Have Met To Worship

William Moore
arr. by Gail Smith

* This is a **grace note** and is sounded very quickly before the chord.

Just one chord is needed to harmonize with the melody. Try playing the chord these other ways:

O The Deep, Deep Love Of Jesus

Thomas J. Williams
arr. by Gail Smith

O The Deep, Deep Love Of Jesus

Thomas J. Williams
arr. by Gail Smith

Love Lifted Me

Howard E. Smith
arr. by Gail Smith

Rock Of Ages

Thomas Hastings
arr. by Gail Smith

For The Beauty Of The Earth

Conrad Kocher
arr. by Gail Smith

Jesus, Lover Of My Soul

Joseph Parry
arr. by Gail Smith

Come, Thou Fount Of Every Blessing

Traditional American Melody
arr. by Gail Smith

Introducing Cadences

Cadences create a sense of repose or resolution at the end of a melodic or harmonic phrase. The strength and finality vary according to the chords used.

Here are the different kinds:

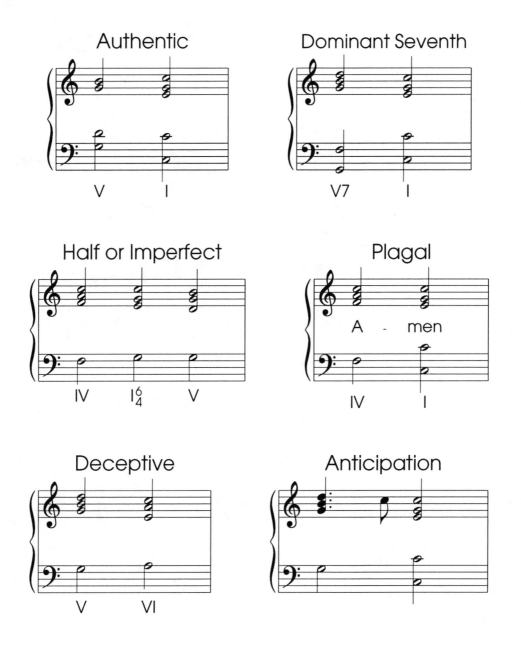

Chapter 7

You can learn the following 88 patterns for the left hand and use them to play gospel songs. There are over twenty hymns in this chapter to show you how to apply these 88 patterns.

88 Left-Hand Patterns

For additional left-hand fills, order a copy of *The Complete Book of Improvisation, Fills and Chord Progressions* by Gail Smith, published by Mel Bay.

The Battle Hymn Of The Republic

He's Got The Whole World In His Hands

Spiritual

Bass pattern #1

He Is Lord

Moderato

mf

Pattern #33

Jesus Loves Me

arr. by Gail Smith

Just As I Am

William Bradbury
arr. by Gail Smith

Pattern #29

When The Roll Is Called

James M. Black
arr. by Gail Smith

Pattern #58

Pattern #59

8va - - - - - - -

Nothing But The Blood

Robert Lowry
arr. by Gail Smith

Standing On The Promises

R. Kelso Carter
arr. by Gail Smith

Glory To His Name

John H. Stockton
arr. by Gail Smith

My Country, 'Tis Of Thee

Samuel F. Smith, 1832

arr. by Gail Smith

America The Beautiful

Pass Me Not, O Gentle Savior

William H. Doane
arr. by Gail Smith

Pattern #73

The dominant seven chord in the key of F is C Dominant Seven:

"Softly And Tenderly" contains two other dominant seven chords. We call these chords "secondary-dominant" chords. They sound like dominant sevens but belong to other keys. Think of these chords as just visiting this key and not living there.

These are the two chords to listen for:

Softly And Tenderly

Will L. Thompson
arr. by Gail Smith

Morning Song

Gaelic Melody
arr. by Gail Smith

Pattern #49

Amazing Grace

Traditional
arr. by Gail Smith

At Calvary

Daniel B. Towner, 1895
arr. by Gail Smith

Silent Night

Franz Gruber
arr. by Gail Smith

Away In A Manger

James R. Murray
arr. by Gail Smith

Pattern #35   Pattern #33   Pattern #28

The First Noel

English Carol
arr. by Gail Smith

What Child Is This

Greensleeves
arr. by Gail Smith

In this next gospel song, we use several left-hand patterns. Chords and patterns are adjusted to sound just right with the melody.

The F Major chord is played these six different ways to fit the melody:

Practice these patterns, then play the arrangement of "Trust And Obey." When you can play it well, try playing the right hand in octaves.

Trust And Obey

Daniel B. Towner
arr. by Gail Smith

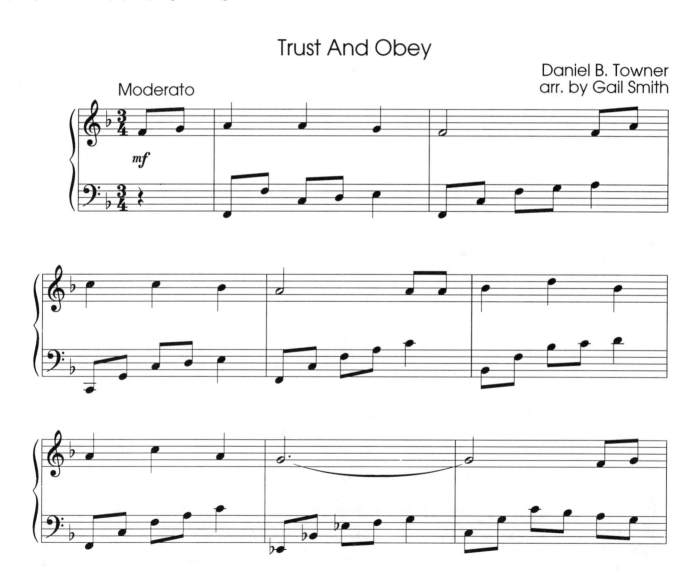

Holy, Holy, Holy

John Dykes
arr. by Gail Smith

Chapter 8

Common Meter, Long Meter, and **Short Meter-16 are determined by the words of the hymn.**
Count the number of syllables in each phrase and that will give you the meter.

Example 1. Common Meter - 8 6 8 6

Oh God, our help in ages past,	*8 syllables*
Our hope for years to come,	*6 syllables*
Our shelter from the stormy blast,	*8 syllables*
And our eternal home!	*6 syllables*

O God, Our Help In Ages Past
St. Anne

Psalm 90
Isaac Watts, 1719

William Croft, 1708

O God, Our Help In Ages Past
St. Anne

William Croft
arr. by Gail Smith

Common meter 8 6 8 6

Example 2. Short Meter - 6 6 8 6

Blest be the tie that binds	*6 syllables*
Our hearts in Christian love;	*6 syllables*
The fellowship of kindred minds	*8 syllables*
Is like to that above.	*6 syllables*

Blest Be The Tie That Binds
Dennis

John Fawcett, 1739/40-1817

Melody by J.G. Nägeli, 1768–1836
Adopted by Lowell Mason, 1792-1872

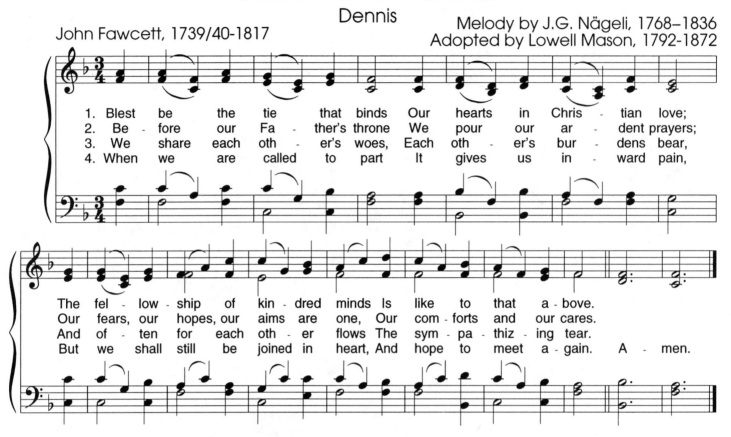

1. Blest be the tie that binds Our hearts in Chris - tian love;
2. Be - fore our Fa - ther's throne We pour our ar - dent prayers;
3. We share each oth - er's woes, Each oth - er's bur - dens bear,
4. When we are called to part It gives us in - ward pain,

The fel - low - ship of kin - dred minds Is like to that a - bove.
Our fears, our hopes, our aims are one, Our com - forts and our cares.
And of - ten for each oth - er flows The sym - pa - thiz - ing tear.
But we shall still be joined in heart, And hope to meet a - gain. A - men.

Blest Be The Tie That Binds
Dennis

Short Meter 6 6 8 6

Lowell Mason

Example 3. Long Meter - 8 8 8 8

Praise God from whom all blessings flow;	*8 syllables*
Praise Him, all creatures here below;	*8 syllables*
Praise Him above, ye heav'nly host;	*8 syllables*
Praise Father, Son, and Holy Ghost.	*8 syllables*

Praise God From Whom All Blessings
Old 100th

The Doxology

Chapter 9
Right-Hand Patterns

The following seven fills are used in the next several gospel songs:

The Lord's My Shepherd, I'll Not Want

Scottish Psalter

Now play the song again, and add this fill for F, C, or G when the right hand has a half note:

Fill #1

This is how you'll start in the right hand:

Oh, How I Love Jesus

Early American Melody
arr. by Gail Smith

R.H. Fill #4

Jesus Never Fails

arr. by Gail Smith

mf

R.H. Fill #7

Only Trust Him

John H. Stockton
arr. by Gail Smith

Day By Day Medley

Swedish Hymn
arr. by Gail Smith

The Two-Beat Fill for the Right Hand

When a half note or two quarter notes on the same pitch are followed by a note a step up, you may fill in the two beats with a scale up to the melody note an octave higher. Or when a half note or two quarter notes are followed by a note a step down, you may fill in the two beats with a scale down to the next melody note an octave lower.

Here are two examples of this kind of fill:

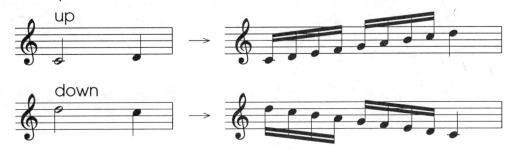

In the next song, number each place you can use this fill. The first 4 are done for you.

Like A River Glorious

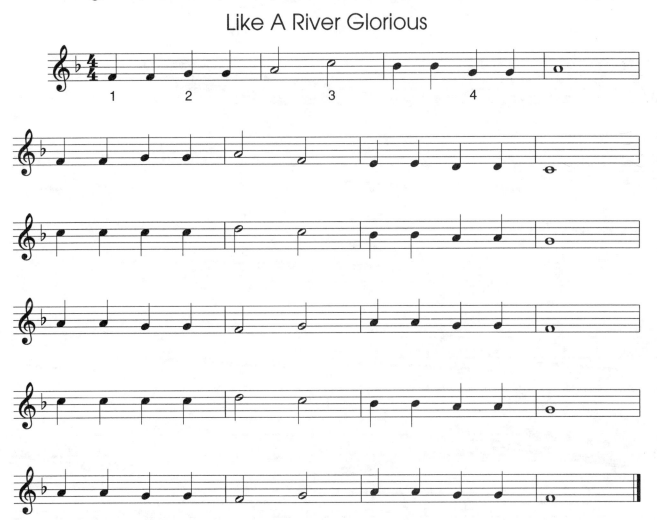

On the next two pages you will see some of the fills written out. How many did you find?

Like A River Glorious

James Mountain
arr. by Gail Smith

105

My Jesus I Love Thee

A.J. Gordon
arr. by Gail Smith

What A Friend

Charles C. Converse
arr. by Gail Smith

Angels We Have Heard On High

French Carol
arr. by Gail Smith

2-beat fill

Jesus! What A Friend Of Sinners
(Hyfrydol 8787)

Rowland H. Prichard
arr. by Gail Smith

*Three-beat fill: Go to the note a fifth higher than the note of the next measure, and play down from there:

The Octave-Jump Fill for the Right Hand

This pattern can be used in gospel songs to fill in between two beats followed by the same note:

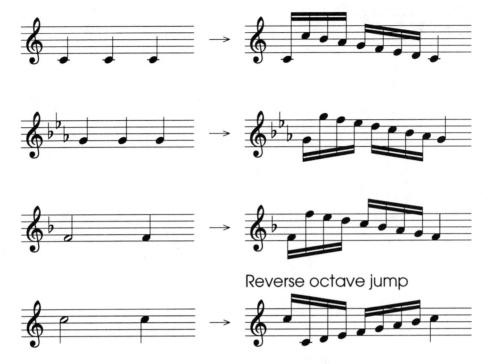

You will always land on the correct note when you play this octave jump followed by a scale!

Abide With Me

William H. Monk
arr. by Gail Smith

Thanksgiving Hymn

Kremser
arr. by Gail Smith

Moderato

octave jump

rit.

114

Four-Beat Fills

To use the chart below, determine the distance between the two notes, then select the four-beat fill accordingly.

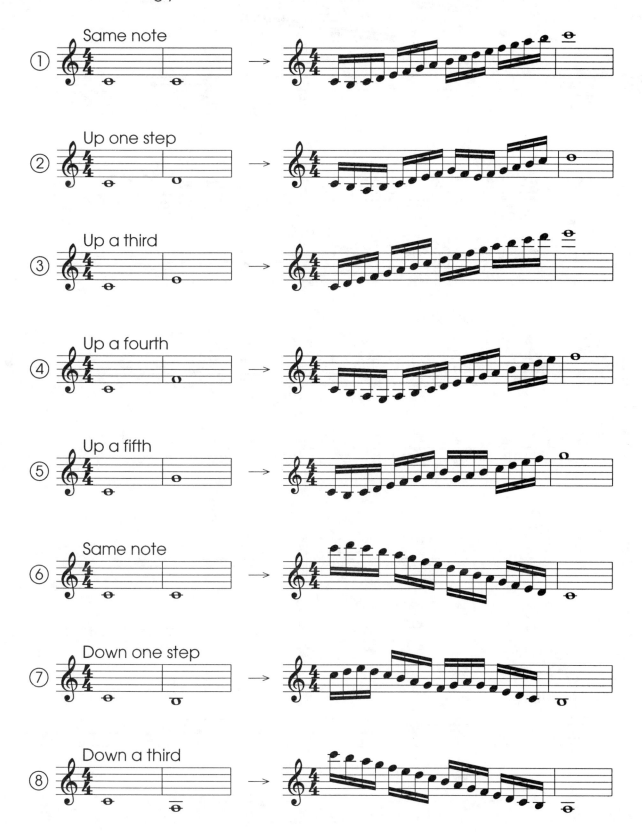

"Onward Christian Soldiers" on the next page has many whole notes in it that can be filled in with the Four-Beat Fill.

Onward Christian Soldiers

Arthur S. Sullivan
arr. by Gail Smith

*When you have four beats and the note in the next measure is a third higher, you play a two-octave scale up to that note:

Chapter 10
Special Effects for the Pianist

Chimes: The right hand plays an interval of a 4th. The left hand plays an interval of a 6th. Both hands have the same melody note on top.

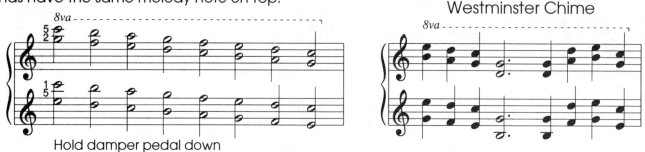

Westminster Chime

Hold damper pedal down

Polytonality: The simultaneous use of two or more tonalities. This chord ending has also been called the "Petrushka Chord," since Stravinsky first used it in that composition.

Tremolo: This is the rapid alternation of two notes, generally an octave apart. This produces a very dramatic effect when the damper pedal is held down. This effect was first written and used in a piano composition by Carl Maria von Weber in his Sonata in A♭, Op. 39. He was born in 1786 and was a child prodigy. His father was the uncle of Mozart's wife. Thus he and Mozart were first cousins by marriage.

Written   Played

Hold pedal down

Introducing Harmonic and Melodic Intervals

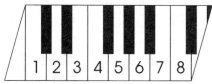

Harmonic intervals - 2 tones played together

2nd   3rd   4th   5th⁻   6th   7th   octave

Melodic intervals - 2 tones played separately

2nd   3rd   4th   5th   6th   7th   octave

Church Chimes

Church Mode
Lowel Mason

* "15va" means play two octaves higher than written.

119

Joy To The World

George Friedrick Handel
arr. by Gail Smith

Christ The Lord Is Risen Today

Easter Hymn 7777
arr. by Gail Smith

The Diminished Chord

The diminished chord may be used as a substitution chord to change the harmony when the chord would remain the same otherwise.

All twelve diminished chords really boil down to only three! The others are all inversions of the first three chords. Here are those three main chords (C, D, and E) and all their inversions:

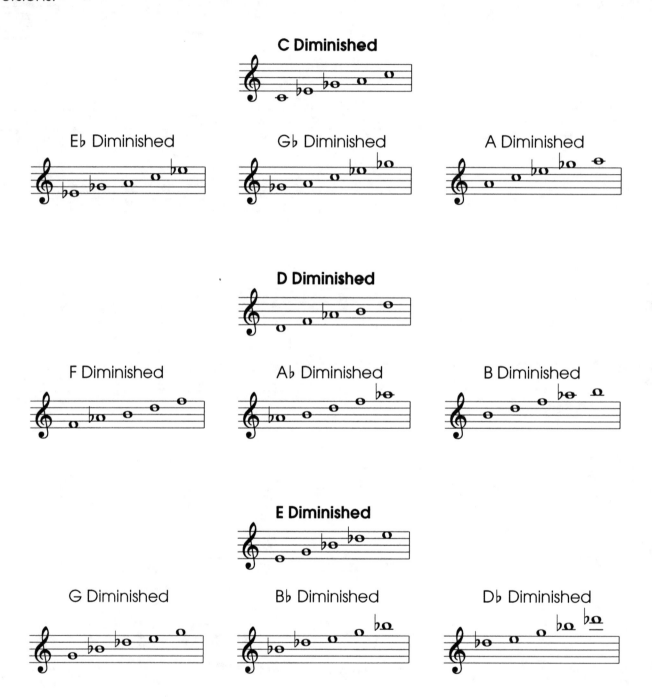

Sweet Hour Of Prayer

William B. Bradbury
arr. by Gail Smith

Continue the dim.
chord into the R.H.

Cdim

*Substitution chord:

Whatever the melody note is, use that diminished chord. It's that simple.

Arranging Tips
Come Thou Almighty King
In Five Different Settings

① **Chimes:** Perfect 4ths in Right Hand, Major 6ths in Left Hand

② **Modern Harmony:** Perfect 4ths

③ **Melody in Bass**

④ **Change of Meter**

⑤ **Change of Mode:** G Minor - parallel minor

Congratulations! You have completed all the songs in this book. Keep reviewing the pieces and try to memorize several of your favorite gospel songs.

You may find it extremely helpful now to purchase my book, *The Complete Book of Improvisation, Chord Progressions & Fills,* published by Mel Bay Publications. Try to learn all the different fills in that book and apply them to your favorite hymns. Also, you might like to play the arrangements in my book, *Country Gospel Songs For Piano Solo.*

Until we meet at a workshop or church concert, take care and God Bless You.

GAIL SMITH

Great Music at Your Fingertips